When Jesus Was Born
The Story of the Very First Christmas

Written and Illustrated by

Magdalena Kim, FSP

Pauline
BOOKS & MEDIA

Boston

Library of Congress Cataloging-in-Publication Data

Kim, Magdalena.
   [Birthday of the Child Jesus]
   When Jesus was born : the story of the very first Christmas / written and illustrated by
Magdalena Kim ; translated from the Korean by Gratia Chang ; edited by Patricia Edward
Jablonski.
         p. cm.
Originally published: The Birthday of the Child Jesus. Seoul, Korea : Daughters of St. Paul, 1998.
   ISBN 0-8198-8297-6 (pbk.)
   1.   Jesus Christ—Nativity—Juvenile literature. [1. Jesus Christ—Nativity.   2. Christmas.]
I. Jablonski, Patricia E.   II. Title.
   BT315.2 .K52 2001
   232.92—dc21

                                                                          00-011781

Translated from the Korean by Gratia Chang, FSP
Edited and adapted by Patricia Edward Jablonski, FSP

Original edition title: *The Birthday of the Child Jesus*

Copyright © 1998, Daughters of St. Paul/Korea
Published by Pauline, 103 Mia-9dong Kangbuk-gu, 142-704 Seoul, Korea
All rights reserved.

English edition copyright © 2001, Daughters of St. Paul/U.S.A.

Illustrations copyright © 1998, Daughters of St. Paul/Korea

Printed and published in the U.S.A. by Pauline Books & Media, 50 Saint Pauls Avenue, Boston, MA
02130-3491.

www.pauline.org

Pauline Books & Media is the publishing house of the Daughters of St. Paul, an international congre-
gation of women religious serving the Church with the communications media.

   2 3 4 5 6   06 05 04 03 02

A long, long time ago, in a village called Nazareth, there lived a young lady named Mary.

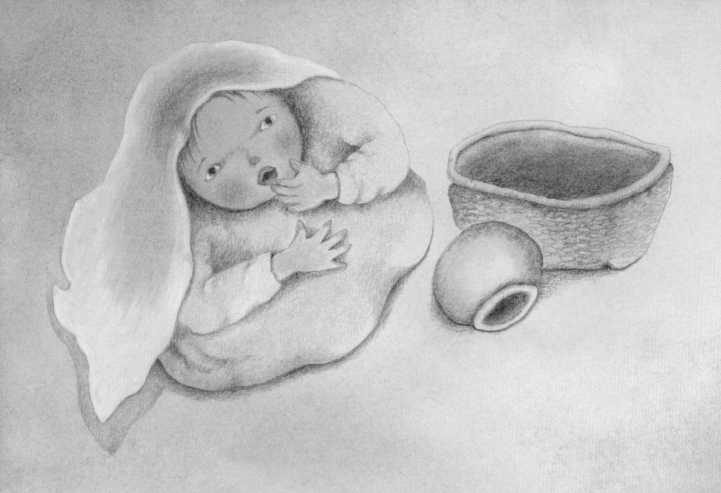

One day, God sent an angel to see Mary. The angel told her, "Mary, God is very pleased with you. You will have a baby, and you will name him Jesus. He will be great and will be called the Son of God."

9

B ut I'm not married to Joseph yet," Mary said. "How can I have a baby?"

"God will make it happen through his power," the angel told her.

Joseph didn't know what to do when he heard this news. *Now that Mary is going to have a baby, I can't marry her,* he thought. *It's against our Jewish law.*

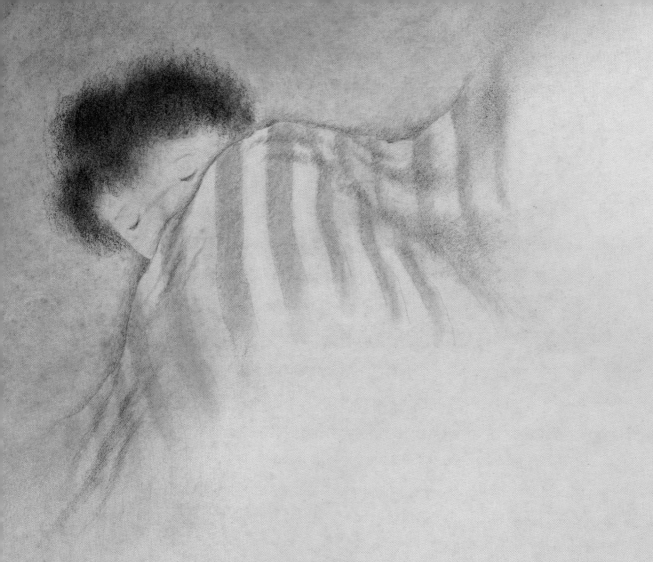

Then an angel appeared to Joseph in a dream. The angel said, "Joseph, don't worry. Mary's baby comes from God. He will save the world."

Joseph was happy again. Now he could marry Mary.

After that Mary and Joseph had to obey the emperor and go to the city of Bethlehem.

Clip-clop, clippity-clop went their little donkey. He was getting tired. It was a long trip.

"We'll soon be in Bethlehem," Joseph said to Mary.

17

Finally, Mary and Joseph had to go to a place where animals lived. This is where Jesus was born.

"Moo! Moo!" said the cow. "Welcome, Baby Jesus!"

"Heehaw! Heehaw!" said the donkey. "I want to say welcome, too!"

"Meow! Meow!" said the cat. "Baby Jesus has come!"

The little lamb and pig were also happy to greet Jesus.

Out in the fields, an angel appeared to some shepherds. "Don't be afraid," the angel told them. "I have good news! Your Savior has been born in Bethlehem! You'll find him lying in a manger."

Suddenly, many other angels also appeared, praising God.

After the angels went away, the shepherds cried, "Let's hurry to see the Savior!" And they ran with their lambs to Bethlehem.

23

24

A big, bright star was shining in the sky. Three wise men, who studied the stars, shouted, "Look at that big star! It means that a king has been born!"

The three wise men hurried to follow the star. It led them on a long trip.

King Herod found out about the three wise men. He asked them, "Has the baby who will become king been born?"

"Yes," the wise men answered.

King Herod said, "When you find this baby, give him my greetings. Then come back and tell me where he is."

But secretly, Herod was thinking, *There has to be only one king, and that's me! I'll have to kill this baby.*

28

The star led the three wise men to Baby Jesus, Mary, and Joseph.

"Jesus, I give you gold as my gift."

"Jesus, I give you myrrh as my gift."

"Jesus, I give you frankincense as my gift."

The wise men gave Baby Jesus the special gifts they had brought.

Then an angel again appeared to Joseph in a dream. The angel said, "Joseph, you have to leave here. King Herod is trying to kill Baby Jesus."

And so Joseph took Jesus and Mary to Egypt.

Finally, King Herod died. Then Joseph brought Jesus and Mary home to Nazareth.

Jesus grew to be the same age as you. He loved and prayed to God his Father. He loved and obeyed Mary his mother and Joseph his foster father. He had fun playing with his friends.

And the town of Nazareth was full of joy and peace.
When he was a young man, Jesus left Nazareth. He
traveled to many cities and towns teaching people about
God his Father. Later, Jesus died on the cross to save us from
our sins. He did this because he loves us so much. But Jesus
is God, and he came back to life again.

Pauline
BOOKS & MEDIA

The Daughters of St. Paul operate book and media centers at the following addresses. Visit, call or write the one nearest you today, or find us on the World Wide Web, www.pauline.org.

CALIFORNIA
3908 Sepulveda Blvd., Culver City, CA 90230;
  310-397-8676
5945 Balboa Ave., San Diego, CA 92111;
  858-565-9181
46 Geary Street, San Francisco, CA 94108;
  415-781-5180

FLORIDA
145 S.W. 107th Ave., Miami, FL 33174;
  305-559-6715

HAWAII
1143 Bishop Street, Honolulu, HI 96813;
  808-521-2731
  Neighbor Islands call: 800-259-8463

ILLINOIS
172 North Michigan Ave., Chicago, IL 60601;
  312-346-4228

LOUISIANA
4403 Veterans Memorial Blvd., Metairie, LA 70006;
  504-887-7631

MASSACHUSETTS
Rte. 1, 885 Providence Hwy., Dedham, MA 02026;
  781-326-5385

MISSOURI
9804 Watson Rd., St. Louis, MO 63126;
  314-965-3512

NEW JERSEY
561 U.S. Route 1, Wick Plaza, Edison, NJ 08817;
  732-572-1200

NEW YORK
150 East 52nd Street, New York, NY 10022;
  212-754-1110
78 Fort Place, Staten Island, NY 10301;
  718-447-5071

OHIO
2105 Ontario Street (at Prospect Ave.), Cleveland,
  OH 44115; 216-621-9427

PENNSYLVANIA
9171-A Roosevelt Blvd., Philadelphia, PA 19114;
215-676-9494

SOUTH CAROLINA
243 King Street, Charleston, SC 29401;
  843-577-0175

TENNESSEE
4811 Poplar Ave., Memphis, TN 38117;
  901-761-2987

TEXAS
114 Main Plaza, San Antonio, TX 78205;
  210-224-8101

VIRGINIA
1025 King Street, Alexandria, VA 22314;
  703-549-3806

CANADA
3022 Dufferin Street, Toronto, Ontario, Canada
  M6B 3T5; 416-781-9131
1155 Yonge Street, Toronto, Ontario, Canada
  M4T 1W2; 416-934-3440

¡También somos su fuente para libros, videos y música en Español!